children only
by Jeannette Altherr

Author: Jeannette Alther   Editor: Carles Broto   Photographies: Olga Carretero.   Photographies (Ternura-Evolución, 00, 01): Giulio Oriani/Vega MG   Grafic design: Laura Armet   Texts: Jeannette Altherr, Teresa Ricard, Bernardo Quiroga   Production: Francisco Orduña   Editorial assistant: Jacobo Krauel
© Carles Broto i Comerma (except Spanish language)   Ausias Marc 20, 4-2 08010 BARCELONA   Tel. 34 933 012 199   Fax. 34 933 026 797.   e-mail:info@linksbooks.net
No part of this publication may be reproduced, stored inretrieval system or transmitted in any forms or means, electronic, mechanical, photocopying, recording or otherwise, without the prior written permission of the owner of the Copyright.

My parents always decide for me…

Whether we're talking about a whole room's conception and decor, or just a stuffed toy, designing for kids is an opportunity, and at the same time a responsibility. Each object in the environment reflects on our part a certain attitude toward the child, and to some extent speaks also of the designers of these objects and their childhood. This is evident above all in those things or spaces created by designers for their own children: here the objects are not mass-produced and so are filled with spontaneity and freedom, a loving subjectivity. The creators, returning to their own childhoods, become a conduit for the flow of past into future.

This book is a 'dream store', a collection of things we would like at least to browse through when thinking of our children. At the same time it is a tour, guided by children themselves, through some habitats where these things might go. And those living spaces have been carefully selected, they are homes belonging to people who prefer to go outside the commercially available range of choices— originals, you might say.

Let's face it —all too often, though we talk about design for children, when it comes to buying things for children's rooms, it's always the adults who choose. Naturally we love and respect our children, but while we recognize that a child could be just as happy playing with an old log, which in the imagination can be anything from a horse to a tightrope, the same child can become just as infatuated with a Barney or Tellytubby doll.

The child is for us a blank page, in which we inscribe our values, beliefs and interests, hoping that at least some of them will stay etched there forever. This process is at work too in the things with which we surround the child. Of course the child will one day make independent choices. Starting —we hope— from the basic values which we have shared with them, our children will create a separate identity for themselves. In this process they will assimilate all kinds of things from their environment —including those things which we parents may wish to reject, sometimes.

Ten chapters, ten families, gathering a concept of living around themselves, as expressed in their homes, and in a variety of objects charged with personal significance. Of course, the choice of objects and spaces featured here is a representative sample from among this dazzling variety. Naturally the 'frontiers' between these life concepts are diffuse and blurry, and some of the objects may slot just as easily into another way of life. Reality, and most especially people's subjective reality, is never quite as tidily categorized as our neat ideas would suggest. As children grow and develop, their needs evolve, and along with their needs, our attitudes toward them are transformed. To cuddle and coddle, to laugh and learn, to share and take turns, to hold and to let go —there is a time for all these moments. There are as many ways to love our children as there are ways to express this love in the space we create for him.

I hope this book does justice to the creativity of that love.   **Jeannette Alther.**

archetype

synthesis

Hannah, Lena. Hannah, Lena. Almost a third of this large old urban apartment, 300 square meters in area, is occupied by these two sisters, four and six years old. They share a bedroom, a small bathroom and a huge games room (originally their father's workroom). Here, the big attraction is a children's playhouse with two floors, made to the girls' size. The design was created by both parents, the mother an architect and the father a designer. Design: Julia Schulz-Dornburg (Germany) and Niall O'Flynn (Ireland)

"We wanted to reduce this space, formerly a study for working, to children's size, but without breaking it up into little rooms. So we had the idea of a house-within-a-house, something like "Alice in Wonderland". The adult, peering in through the upper floor windows, seems like a giant to those inside. It's the archetypal house, though this time in a contemporary urban style."

"The playhouse can be enjoyed as much on the outside, to be climbed over, as on the inside, where it is a completely equipped house in miniature. It contains everything you would expect: a kitchen, a dining-room, a living room and upstairs, a bedroom. This children's playhouse has an important symbolic function, much more than a mere room in the house. Here the girls have their own space, it's a 'chill-out zone' where adults are not admitted. Moreover, it's a structural element: as the centre of the room, they play both in front of and behind it, the rug acts as a lawn, and they can run all around it, without it losing its character as an 'object'. It's like a synthesis of all the houses where we parents lived as children."

This "mobile kid's office" is moved wherever it is needed and is used to keep artistic materials and other things. There is a continual fluid interchange between the girls' world and the world of their parents, which spills over into the working world: the children leave their traces in their mother's study when they come in to look for 'supplies' or use the photocopier. The footprint is the newly-born Hannah's, which was used for invitations to her christening.

Aquacolor. Functionalist and spare in conception and outline, this paintbox hides a secret: open the outer covering, and you have a container for water which you can carry by the sealing clasp. A pure and sophisticated approach to a functional need, resolved with clarity and simplicity.

01

Designer: Emilio Ambasz, 1985   Maker: Herlite (Germany)   Materials: Injection-molded polystyrene   Dimensions: 22.6 x 9.3 x 3.3 cm

This central theme of the home appears in other places too. For example, here we see one of Hannah's models, which imitates an architectural model made by her mother. We can see a synthesis of the things that matter to her in the original: the facade, the swimming pool, the owner and the flag.

The kitchen counter is of slate, a material often used as a bar-top in England and Ireland, as it is durable and you can also note down the bar tab in chalk on top of it. As the girls spend a lot of time in the kitchen, they entertain themselves by drawing among the tomatoes and onions.

In Hannah and Lena's room there's a wall which is being steadily covered by images: paintings, drawings, and photos of friends and relatives.

Drawing Table. The Dutch partnership Droog Design are noted for their creation of objects with unusual combinations of uses, a double meaning sometimes achieving the poetic. What do chalkboards and dining tables have in common? Answer: you can draw on both of them. This object synthesizes both things, becoming a knowing wink to children from the adult world.

Designer: Djonke de Joong for DROOG Design, 1994   Maker: DMD (Holland)   Materials: Plywood coatted with matt black 'slate' effect paint.   Dimensions: 50 x 75 x 58 cm

Sleeping Bag. From their own experiences as mothers, the designers have conjured up this multifunctional object: in the cradle or the buggy, a sleeping bag; when unzipped, a play-rug with teething ring, rattle and interesting tactile sensations to experience.

Designer: Terry Pecora, Marian de Rond, 1995   Maker: Prenatal (Italy)   Materials: Exterior covering nylon, inner lining 100% cotton

Bart. The most minimal expression possible of a bed's form. The mattress is supported on wooden boards and the frame can be simply folded to form a sofa, Turkish divan-style. The bed grows with a child from first infancy to teen years, adapting at the same time to the changing profile of a child's room as bedroom, study and space to 'hang out'.

04

Designer: Vico Magistretti, 1994   Maker: Flou (Italy)   Materials: Wooden frame with steel rollers. Cotton coverings.   Dimensions: 110 x 200 x 50 cm

Inter-action. A piece which is both furniture and plaything, these cushions are designed for two people to enjoy. Once inflated, we see the "umbilical cord" connecting the two cushions; this functions so that whatever one person does is felt by the other, sitting in the cushion's twin.

06...

Designer: Martin Azúa, 2001   Materials: Inflatable plastic   Dimensions: Each cushion 60 x 60 cm

humour

colour

Maria. Maria. In this city apartment, dating from 1870, inherited by the present owners – he an architect, she a graphic designer – who reformed the place thoroughly. Their daughter Maria, eighteen months old, has a small bedroom and a play area in an alcove in one of the shared family spaces. Design: Gustavo Gilli and Eulalia Coma (Spain)

The apartment forms a series of seven rooms connecting with the neighboring spaces, giving the place a true "loft" feel. As it faces north, it has been painted entirely white, alternating with intense warm colors such as red, orange and yellow to balance the cold whiteness. These tones are repeated like a motif throughout the home, highlighting and defining spaces such as the child's play area or the kitchen. The color scheme suggests a Mediterranean air, but interpreted this time in a modern and graphical way.

Rondini. A paintbox designed for children from three to six years of age. The paint containers are large enough to be easily gripped by young fingers, and the lids can also be used as containers for water. The set is of a few basic colours so that the children can learn to make their first blends of color. A "basket of eggs" and an eternal invitation to get painting.

Designer: Yellow Circle, 1998   Maker: Pelikan (Germany)   Materials: Moulded polystyrene.   Dimensions: 14 x 24 x 4 cm

Maria's bedroom is equipped with a barred crib, a bed for the babysitter, and plasterboard shelf unit which also serves as a closet. Instead of a door to the room there is a sliding screen, which offers privacy whenever necessary.

Each room has an alcove, forming a more intimate zone. In one of them a kitchen was placed, in another a play area for Maria. In the careful way it has been laid out, we note the hand of the graphic artist mother: the toy boxes are transparent, and tidily formed in rows along the wall. At the top of each one, at the height of Maria's eyes, is a sketch representing various friends and relatives. And because the family thought of this place as a 'park' for Maria, it was only natural that they would want to install a swing there too. The same trick of repetition is to be seen on the floor, which is really a foam-rubber jigsaw puzzle in various colors. This common toy was bought in wholesale quantities so that the family could achieve a wall-to-wall effect in a floor covering that was soft, easy-to-clean and colorful. This area is part of a room shared by all the family, as can be appreciated by the sight of Maria's little chair and table among the adult armchairs. On the walls, her drawings are proudly hung. "Now we're expecting another baby, and we know everything will change, but we don't know quite how. No problem — these are very flexible spaces."

Agata. Between pop art and naive art, the chairs designed by Agatha Ruiz de la Prada are there to define the child's space with a form that appears to have been cut from paper by the children themselves. They work just as well standing alone or in combination, with repetitions and restatements of shapes and color.

02

Designer: Agatha Ruiz de la Prada, 1996   Maker: Amat3 (Spain)   Materials: Tubular steel frame with seat and seat back in laminated ply board. Dimensions: 41 x 43 x 69 cm   A matching table, in the form of a floating cloud, is also available.

1, 2, 3 Inspired by the story "Goldilocks and the Three Bears", with the three bowls of large, medium and small size, this set of dishes comes complete with wooden spoon and bib. The design motif is like something sketched in coloured pencil; a cultured design which becomes a universal symbol.

03

Designer: Virginia Pulm, 1996   Maker: Aguadó (Spain)   Materials: Bone colored ceramic with coloured glazes in blue, ochre and green.
Dimensions: Small: 8.5 cm in diameter x 6.5 cm height; Medium: 15.5 cm diameter x 5 cm height; Large: 20 cm in diameter x 2.5 cm height.

Zebra. With all of the charm of children's sketches, these minimalist zebras —the animal formed from just a few strokes of black— are repeated going to and fro, like lambs jumping a fence. What seems from afar like an abstract array of lines becomes, on closer inspection, a touching and intelligible image.

04

Designer: Niroko Hiroshiga, 1995   Maker: Kinnasand (Germany)   Materials: 100% cotton

ABC. A tricycle and a scooter that combine basic shapes and colours. They seem to be inspired by construction sets, a design taken from the didactic world, as suggested by the name. Four black poles and a few colorful geometric shapes, like a Miró sculpture on wheels.

05

Designer: Pineau & LePurcher, 1992   Maker: Italtrike (Italy)   Materials: Painted steel tube and PVC colour components.
Dimensions: 30 cm length x 34 cm height

Loveables. Everyone who has children knows that they spend a lot of time on the floor, and that that means a lot of spilled orange juice and other substances not so easy to clean. The designer of these machine-washable rugs has achieved a design so simple you would think the child had sketched it on the floor.

06...

Designer: Agatha Ruiz de la Prada, 1999   Maker: Nani Marquina (Spain)   Materials: Machine-washable acrylic fiber   Dimensions: 60 x 90 cm, 70 x 140 cm, 80 x 100 cm

tenderness

evolution

Laura. A young designer and her family live and work in this two-story rural house. On the ground floor are the carpentry and textile workshops, and on the upper floor the family's rooms. The daughter, Laura, only three months old, still sleeps with her parents and has no room of her own. Design: Katrin Arens and Omero Gasparetti (Italy)

The house, with its milky walls, is redolent of the owner's particular perfume, a woman who works to unite her personal and professional lives by creating a bridge between past and present. She lives with her family in a universe of her own making, surrounded by objects she has made herself. Her work is to renew old wooden materials, creating new things that bear the stamp of time in their fabric. It is a philosophy which is at one and the same time loving toward the past and critical of contemporary consumerist society, which moves fast with little time for nostalgia.

"I've always been passionate about 'poor' materials and cast-offs. For many years I've been taking unwanted timber from construction sites and derelict houses, and I love to make them live again in a new context. The fun is in transforming something unwanted into an object with an intention."

For instance, for her daughter Laura, she has made a rocking crib out of an old barrel, a changing table, and a crib with bars, bearing inscriptions in pencil from "The Little Prince" by Antoine Saint-Exupery (for when she can read them). As with the rest of the wooden objects in the house, they are treated with an old craft technique which weathers them, leaving them looking like pieces of driftwood washed up on the beach.

"Laura will sleep in our room until she's three at least, because we know that small children need to be where their parents are. Instead of a room of her own, she'll have a corner of her own in every room in the house. In our room, she has her bed and her books; in the workshop, a table and stool to sit on; in the hallway she'll have a roll of paper for drawing; and in the kitchen a tent or a little kitchen all her own..."

Pom, Tita, Hella, Mop. **Cuttings and cast-offs that survive the ravages of time, so that fashions from the past are renewed to appear as something new. These garments, made from the old clothes of adults, embody the idea of transformation of old into new, reconciling the past and the present with a clear anti-consumerist message.**

01

Designer: Katrin Arens, 2000   Maker: Katrin Arens (Italy)   Materials: Fabric offcuts, blankets and used clothing

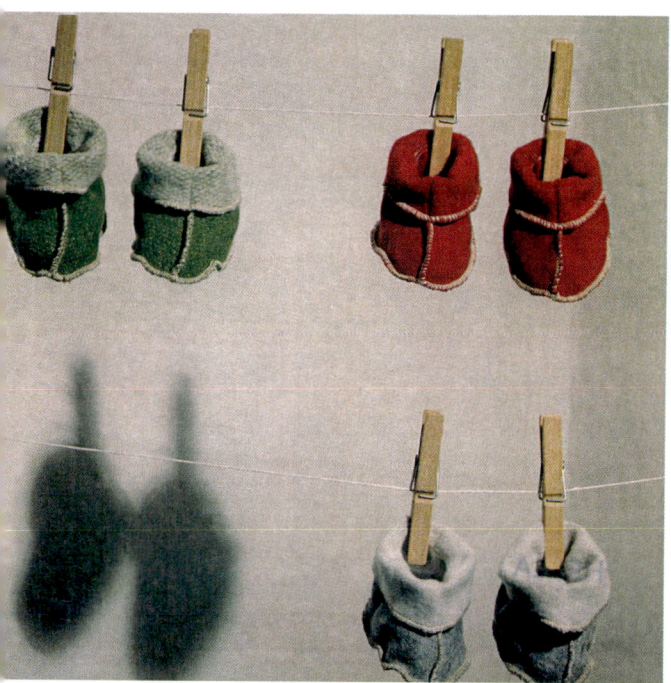

The same philosophy of simplicity which lies behind the furniture in the house was also the driving force for a collection of clothing and accessories for children called VaterMutterKind (FatherMotherChild). The collection is made from old adult clothes and fabric off-cuts, and in practice is fairly evocative of old Shaker designs, with natural colors and materials, rooted in a simple rural life.

Reduced to kid-sized proportions, the designs wear their recycled origins with pride, with old pockets, lapels and cuffs on display. The collection, which at the moment covers children from zero to three years old, has been inspired by the designer's daughter Laura. "The idea for VaterMutterKind started almost as a joke. I began by making shirts and pyjamas for baby Laura, but she goes on growing, and with her the idea..."

What stands out here, as much in the house and its fixtures, as in the clothing Katrin designs, is a respect for the passing of time. "I'd love it if we used things for a thousand years. I feel secure surrounded by objects that tell their own story. And deciding to make a garment for your baby out of our old shirts is another affirmation of this cyclic aspect of our lives. It's almost as if the human warmth remains impregnated in the fabric itself, allowing us to embrace the child by extension."

Puntos. An updating of the craft of embroidery, realised with exquisite delicacy and traditional attention to quality. The idea of creating this range of accessories came from a garment designed by Marta Rodriguez, and the bib forms part of a series that includes towels, sheets and cradle covers. Things which manage to be both timeless and of the moment.

02

Designer: Marta Rodriguez, 1994   Maker: Marta Rodriguez (Spain)   Materials: 100% unshrinkable unbleached cotton, with hand-stitched embroidery in four colours.

A tent mounted on a moses basket, the whole arrangement mounted on wheels. A very useful object not only during the summer months and for trips to the country. With pockets, the coverings are washable. The whole object folds into a compact space. Both nostalgic and functional, at the same time avoiding the obvious clichés.

Designer: Paolo Pellion, 1979   Maker: Art & Form (Italy)   Materials: Frame and wheels in wood. Washable coverings in raw cotton   Dimensions: 106 x 65 x 110 cm

Shoulder craddle. **In many cultures it is believed that close physical contact between parent and child is essential to the child's well-being. Ideal for transporting the newly born child, the form of the cradle adapts itself ergonomically to the parent's body. As close contact is maintained, the child feels safe and protected, guaranteeing a relaxed sleep —all this while the adult can carry out everyday tasks at home or work.**

Designer: Terry Pecora and Marian de Rond, 1997   Maker: Prenatal (Italy)   Materials: Frame and wheels in wood. Washable coverings in raw cotton
Dimensions: 106 x 65 x 110 cm

Notturno Italiano As many children are afraid of the dark, each bedtime can become a weary argument over how many lights to leave on or how many doors to leave open. This magic lamp in the form of a spotlight projects a never-ending parade of lambs, relaxing and lulling the child to sleep.

05...

Designer: Denis Santachiara, 1989   Maker: Domodinamica (Italy)   Materials: Cast aluminum   Dimensions: 16 x 24 17 cm

tradition

change

Lucas, Emma. Lucas, Emma. The same family has lived in this lordly nineteenthcentury townhouse for generations. Today, three generations have their roots here, grandparents, parents and children. Lucas, ten, and Emma, eight, live on the ground floor of this house which their parents, both architects, completely reformed just a few years ago. They each have their own room and share a bathroom. Design: Eileen Liebmann (USA) and Fernando Vilavecchia (Spain)

The few rooms in the house are huge and all-white. "Going into the children's room is like going from the white of the egg into the yolk, an egg-room where something is growing, all right. It's a very high-ceilinged room, and we were worried that the kids would feel lost in so much space. So we decided to give the room kid-sized proportions. Before that, we'd been working a lot with headboards for beds made in white-lacquered plywood, with space behind the board to pass electrical cables, and from this we had the idea of panelling the room, with the panels taking up about a third of the total height. Here we didn't want to paint everything white, but rather in strong colors, but without falling into the cliché of primary colors. Yellow and green had been used in other parts of the house, and red was more complicated to use, but we liked it very much as a background color. The difficult thing in making a room like this is that it was impossible to predict how it would turn out. It also had to be sufficiently neutral so as to be adaptable to changes as the children grew."

In the "before" and "after" photos we can clearly see the changes wrought in this room. Note that the paneled layout of the room allows them to position the beds either in parallel or at an angle.

N 65. A chair in basic form which satisfies functional needs and offers the warmth of wood. The joining of the legs to the chair structure was one of the themes that obsessed Aalto; here the resolution of the four legs is just as in the more famous Stool Number 60 - which features three legs - and is complemented by curved wooden back.

02

Designer: Alvaar Aalto, 1933-35   Maker: Artek (Finland)   Materials: Curved birchwood with optional seating in birch ply or linoleum. Laminated or covered in fabric or leather.   Dimensions: 35 x 38 x 60 cm   In the same range, there is a set of mini tables which can be combined to form a large table.

The children had shared their room up to now, but Emma has just moved to the room next door, formerly the guest room. In this room, apart from hanging the large painting, no work has been done as yet.

Bauhaus. Some years ago, the designer had the idea of creating a doll's house for her niece. "I was thinking about what size it should be – she was growing fast – and what things she would want in it. I couldn't decide, so I let her choose." The result was a modular system with four elements – bedroom, attic, balcony and stairway – which can be fitted together in a variety of ways. A doll's house that manages to be a construction set at the same time.

Designer: Joanna Thomas, 1997   Maker: Joanna Thomas (Spain)   Materials: Recycled cardboard panels which are bought ready for assembly by the child
Dimensions: Basic module 21 x 21 x 14 cm

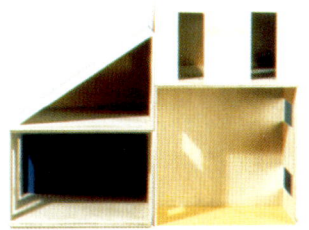

In the hallway is a table, an emblem for the whole family, which holds a collection of souvenirs from various travels, miscellaneous inherited objects – such as the toy soldiers – and things made by the children themselves, such as a section of freeway. "We live in a house passed on to us by our family and shared with our family. We are to be found somewhere between the unchangeable tradition of the past and the unrelenting change of today".

A reinterpretation of a traditional rocking cradle with minimal structure in wood. It has a sheer tulle cover which is complimented by a mosquito net and a bar on which to hang toys. For babies up to six months of age, and can be readily disassembled for easy storage.

Designer: Lievore Altherr Molina, 1998   Maker: Prenatal (Italy)   Materials: Beech wood treated with satin-effect coating, with durable sheer tulle coverings.   Dimensions: 55 x 85 x 68 cm

Crescere. A system of furniture modules designed to grow up with the child right through childhood. The design is formally neutral so that the child has the opportunity to make the pieces originals, something individual for the room instead of commercial designs that get old quickly.

0 – 2 years: A single piece, both cradle and changing station, with shelf space complemented by wooden boxes.

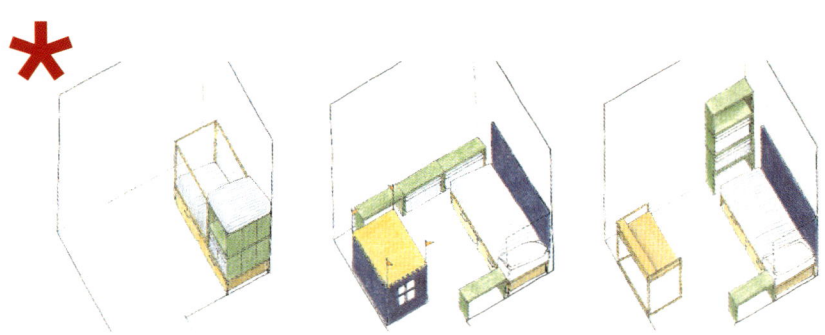

*

Designer: Lievore Altherr Molina, 1998   Maker: Orizzonti (Italy)   Materials: Beech wood treated with wax-effect coating, with durable sheer tulle coverings, 100% cotton available in various colours.   Dimensions: Whole set: 195 x 60 x 80 cm   Bed/House/Table: 195 x 60 x 80 cm   Base/Bed: 195 x 80 x 32 cm   Shelf units: 80 x 26.5 x 30 cm

2 – 6 years: The same pieces, reassembled, become a bed, a playhouse, with shelf units that can form a long low table, a single shelf unit, a night table...

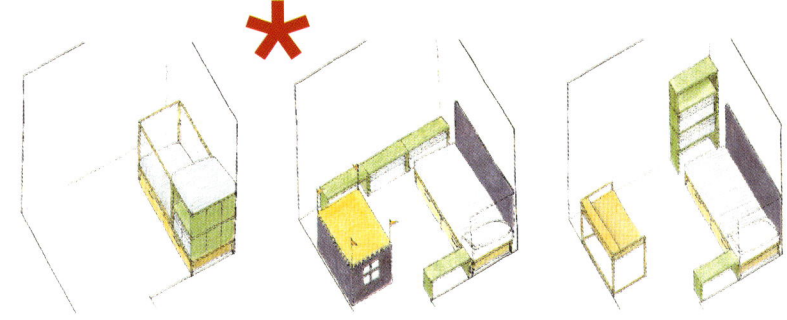

6 years and older: The set is augmented, the playhouse now becomes a desk of adjustable height, the bed can become a sofa in the daytime, and the shelf units can be rearranged at will.

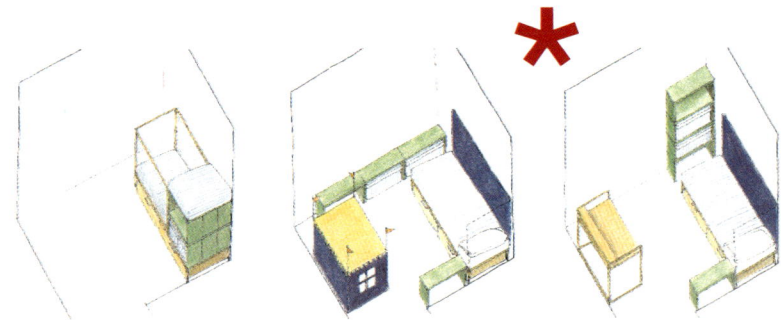

S 43-K. A child size version of the original cantilevered seat, a pioneering object above all in the legal precedent of establishing copyright for an artistic design. An emblem of the functionalist movement, this seat was designed by Mart Stam, guest professor at The Bauhaus in Dessau, and it is a perfect example of a piece from the avant-garde becoming a classic of design.

06...

Designer: Mart Stam, 1927   Maker: Gebrüder Thonet (Germany)   Materials: Frame in chromed tubular steel with seat back and seat in curved wood.
Dimensions: 31 x 40.5 x 61 cm or 40 x 40.5 x 61 cm   There is a matching table as well.

materiality

freedom

Cirilo, Amanda, Matilda. Cirilo, Amanda, Matilda. These three kids, respectively one, four and eight years old, live with their parents (she a translator and he an architect) in a loft apartment in the heart of the old city. It was formerly a refrigerated meat storeroom, which Gustavo turned first into an exhibition space and finally into a home for his family. In doing so, he made use of certain elements of the art gallery, such as the display windows and the moveable light fixtures. Design: Gustavo Barba and Magdelena Martinez (Argentina)

Immediately upon entering, one finds oneself in the kitchen, with a vast wooden table stretching across the space. There is also a huge swivel –chalkboard, which is there both for the children to draw on and to separate this area from that of the kitchen– dining area. "We cut the square hole you see in the chalkboard so that Cirilo, who was just that high at the time, could look through to the other side. Today we use it to hold sticks of chalk."

It is the only feature that functions to close off an area in the whole apartment, a remarkably open space without permanent 'rooms' and almost without doors –the only exception being the door to the bathroom which Magda insisted on having!. "We like everything to be exposed to view, to be open and apparent."

"When we moved here, Cirilo was four years old and had only just started getting on and off the bed by himself. The bed we installed like a bunk bed with a ladder above the bathtub and a couple of closets. Amanda slept below, in a crib. We imagined that when the time came, she would sleep in a bed on rollers that we had made expressly for her, but nothing doing! She preferred to sleep up in the bunk with her brother. There's enough space for two mattresses there, though it is a bit difficult to make the beds in such a cramped space. They climb up the ladder, and get down by sliding down the fireman's pole —the kids love that part, and so do their friends. And when the doors are closed on the bed— nook it becomes a self-contained space, like a cabin or a cave. This feature works especially well, even when we have friends over for dinner. As the children could sleep soundly through an earthquake, the noise of the party doesn't disturb them. Meanwhile, the bed we'd made for Amanda became a family day-bed.

The whole apartment breathes an air of unconventionality, the workings of a free spirit. There is, for instance, a lively interest in invention and objects with double functionality, to be seen in the mobile lighting system, the chalkboard/interior wall, the day-bed, the children's cave/bed, and even a metal car that Gustavo made for the children, adorned with Thai cushions. The niches and display windows which, when the place was a gallery, housed exhibits, now hold plates, candles, souvenirs, and all kinds of objects. Sometimes the children's toys are stored alongside the parents' things, and in one case one of the niches serves as a space to change the youngest one. There is also an interesting mix of materials: sometimes dense and heavy, like the untreated tropical hardwoods of the dining table or the closet doors, or the iron of the toy cars; at others light and transparent, like the glass display cabinets and the brightly-coloured toys.

Tummytub. Startling design for a bathtub which places the baby in a fetal position, reassuring and relaxing for both infant and carer. The design allows the baby to relax unsupported by adult hands, giving a safe and satisfying bathtime for all. Tummytub was designed in conjunction with advice from pediatricians, nurses and midwives.

01

Designer: Domovital, 1998   Maker: Domovital (Germany)   Materials: Translucent PVC, biodegradable and recyclable
Dimensions: 30 cm in diameter x 34 cm high

"Right now we have to say that the apartment is getting a little too small for us. We would like to have a separate room for Cirilo, for instance, so he can listen to the loud music he likes, and within a few years he and Amanda won't want to share a bed any more. We don't have any quiet, private spaces at present. During the weekend that's not too much of a problem, as the kids are at school all day, but at weekends we really miss having a place like that. We wouldn't like to leave this flat: we've put so much of ourselves into it, we love the neighborhood and the views, and we have the park nearby. But we need more living space, simple as that."

Barchetta. This cradle will rock in all directions, as if it were a small piece of floating space. A complex conception is resolved with grace and formal simplicity, evoking the doll's bed made of a shoebox. The original forms part of a collection at the Berliner Kunstgewerbe Museum.

02

Designer: Huub Ubbens, 1995   Maker: Malofancon (Italy)   Materials: Birch plywood with satin-effect coating.   Dimensions: 82 x 60 x 48 cm

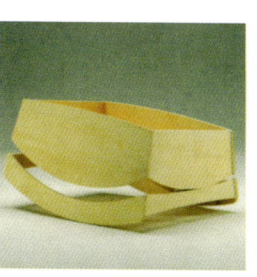

Pillow Play. Full of little foam balls that spell fun, this playful piece of furniture lends itself to play, sleep and relaxation. The texture of the filling, and the crackling sound made, offers novel sensations and the possibilities for use are endless: hammock for the baby, pillow, football... you name it.

Designer: Ana Mir, 1999   Maker: Authentics (Germany)   Materials: Elastic lycra cover with filling of polystryrene 'pearls'.
Dimensions: 40 x 40 cm and 70 x 70 cm

Boxes go to school. The covering of these boxes allows them to be written and painted on as often as their owner wants. The box itself becomes its own 'brand' or 'logo', so it will never be out of fashion. As with all such brilliant ideas, we wonder why nobody had ever thought of it before.

Designer: Curro Claret, 1996   Maker: Curro Claret   Materials: Corrugated cardboard with plastic 'whiteboard' covering.   Dimensions: 20 x 30 x 20 cm

Back Pack. Selecting a bag for the child's things can often be a problematic proposition, most being too large, allowing everything to fall to the bottom and jumble together. This functional and smart backpack is equipped with side pockets for feeding bottles, and handy interior sections to keep things separate. And it goes without saying that the pack isn't just useful for the baby's things...

05

Designer: Terry Pecora and Marian de Rond, 1996   Maker: Prenatal (Italy)   Materials: 100% cotton   Dimensions: 91 x 52 x 55 cm

Literal. This fold-out bed, designed to be fixed to the wall, can be in single or bunk-bed configuration. A great solution to the problem of limited space, all too common in children's rooms. Folded against the wall, it can become a bulletin board for posters, notes and postcards, or as a whiteboard. Inspired by the couchettes of European overnight trains.

Designer: Lievore Altherr Molina, 1997   Maker: Sellex (Spain)   Materials: Tubular steel frame with bed structure in solid birch. Varnish or paint finish optional.   Dimensions: 202 x 90 x 178 cm

magic

memory

Lena Julieta. The designer mother and her daughter share an apartment in a late nineteenth century house. Lena-Julieta, three years old, has a small bedroom which gives onto a tranquil interior patio, and a playroom, more noisy but drenched in sunlight. Design: Jeannette Altherr (Germany)

"I suppose that you are trying to recreate the world of your childhood, though of course filtered through adult consciousness. My home was a mixture of Carl Larson (an artist-architect of the early twentieth century) and love for Mediterranean culture, in a hippie version. It was a large house with an air of magic about it, each room was a different color, intense, full of objects, books and pictures to feed the imagination. In my memories it resembles nothing more that the fantastic house in Ingmar Bergman's "Fanny and Alexander" owned by the Jewish character.

Almost all the furniture in the house is a prototype design, and Lena-Julieta's room is no exception. Her bed is the older version of the crib that she had when she was a baby – the Barquita Crib – which was in turn the reinterpretation of the designer's own childhood bed. "It was old-fashioned, like a boat, with a headboard and a high footboard, and I felt really safe in it. But of course nostalgia like this only makes sense to the person experiencing the memories, it is not transferable to another person. And so it seems that what my daughter really wants is a bunk bed, like the one her friend next door has!"

Barquito. Suggested by a tale in which the protagonist floats up to the moon in a bed/boat, this cradle is an archetype of a toy. For newlyborns to six months, in treated wood finish or with a variety of coverings, and is complemented with a bar to hang a mosquito net or toys.

01

Designer: Lievore Altherr Molina, 1998   Materials: Frame of plywood board. Roller wheels. Rocker in pure beech wood, with cushioned interior and optional cotton cover. Easy to disassemble.   Dimensions: 91 x 52 x 55 cm

The doll house in the playroom was the baby's changing station, and when it was no longer needed, I painted it white and added the roof and doors. Right now it serves above all as a store closet for toys: one of the units is a little kitchen, another is a chest of drawers, with doors and drawers to open and shut, another is an abstract version of a bathroom. "The final unit will be finished in the future, perhaps we'll make it a real dolls house. Or a Barbie-House, who knows? At this age, children don't mind the clash between objects of different scale. It's like in those medieval paintings where enormous human figures coexist on the same plane with tiny ones."

The feature that gives structure to the room is the shelving unit. On one side it is an enormous cork board, painted to match the walls, where we hang photos, postcards, drawings and notes. On the other side it forms the wall of a little alcove, with a mattress for visitors or baby-sitters and a number of scatter cushions to stretch out and read on. "I'm still fascinated by storybooks and children's tales. I remember clearly going to the public library every week to borrow a book, and since then I've bought many of those old stories. In fact, Lena-Julieta has more books than any other toy. As I'm well aware of the fact that it will be me who is reading them to her later, I take care to buy her only those I will enjoy reading as well…"

Luna. The moon is an elemental character in so many stories, the subject of many a rhyme and lullaby. Here the moon becomes a rocking cradle. In 1998 the original of this design was sold in Christies of New York for $18,400, a record for a contemporary original. After this success, which resulted in a flood of orders, the design was issued in limited edition.

02

Designer: Fornasetti, 1995   Maker: Fornasetti (Italy)   Materials: Painted wood with padded interior.   Dimensions: 150 cm diameter x 65 cm height

Her daughter leaves traces of herself all around the home, with books and toys left lying forgotten in the kitchen, the living room, the bathroom or the balcony. "She always ends up playing wherever I happen to be, in my way to an extent, bit that's a good thing, as it allows us to maintain contact even when we're doing our own things. And I love coming across the little surrealist scenes that she creates, like a procession of little animals going down the arm of the chair, or an improvised house under the table. Sometimes these little montages are more revealing about what is going on in her head than what she tells me, and above all they are patches of magic, like small visual poems."

Hoppa. This washable rug is to be walked on, like a sidewalk, without worrying about cleaning your shoes first. And the design, the timeless hopscotch, evokes in us the memory of a time in which to be happy all we needed was a piece of chalk...

03

Designer: Ikea, 1998   Maker: Ikea (Sweden)   Materials: Nylon and polyester   Dimensions: 92 x 200 cm

Baby Chair. The Ditzels designed this when their twin daughters and their older sister were of an age to sit at table. The footrest is adjustable and the bar which secures the infant can be easily detached when the child is able to get up and down without help, so the design develops with the child. A versatile chair for a range of ages, and a sensitive reinterpretation of a classic high-chair design. A fine example of the best of modern Danish design.

04

Designer: Nanna and Jorgen Ditzel, 1956   Maker: Kvist Mobler A/S (Denmark)   Materials: Solid beech wood   Dimensions: 45 x 42 x 71 cm

Casa de Luz. This lamp, based on a rural Spanish cottage, is an archetype devoid of detail, as the designer explains "It is the synthesis or sketch of a childhood dream in sculptural form". Though clearly inspired by the world of the child's imagination, it was not specifically designed for children.

05

Designer: Cristina Figarola, 1998   Maker: Cristina Figarola (Spain)   Materials: Metallic wireframe structure with shades in colored translucent plastic (fully washable).   Dimensions: 24 x 40 x 45 cm. There are three models, of varying size, in the range.

Zigeunerwagen. Children, when they construct little shelters for themselves, are expressing two basic desires: to have adventures, and to feel protected. This "gypsy caravan" contains a bed, closet, desk and shelf unit, which can all also be detached for separate use. The designer of this house-on-wheels, a father himself, has demonstrated that he knows the spirit of the child with this circus-like treat.

Designer: Ulf van Afferden, 1997   Maker: Gunther Lambert (Germany)   Materials: Treated solid pine with details in red lacquer paint
Dimensions: 280 x 111 x 203 cm

abstract

organic

Alba. Alba. Six years old, she lives with her architect parents in a duplex city apartment. Family life courses through the upper floor, a single open space containing the kitchen, dining area, living area and terrace. Downstairs, the bedrooms and bathrooms are all linked by another open space, used as a study, which is shared by all the family. Design: Suzanne Strum (USA) and Rodrigo Diaz (Chile)

"We often have friends by for dinners and parties, just like both of us experienced when we were kids. It's a very open house, in all senses, and it works very well for us because the upstairs/downstairs division helps us psychologically to differentiate the spaces."

The grown-ups usually stay upstairs and the children play downstairs, so that a lot of conversation passes up and down the stairs. Downstairs, Alba has a space where she can do what she likes, with a work table of her own – a simple board with legs from Ikea which we cut down to her size – and a big roll of paper which she can pull out over the table and draw on. We bought the chairs in a street market.
Parents and daughter share the shelf space, with large books on architecture at one end, and storybooks and drawing implements at the other. There's also a collection of souvenirs and trinkets given as presents by friends, which Alba likes to play with – such as the big mask which Rodrigo bought in a Chinese supermarket in Canal Street, New York, because he thought the face reminded him of his daughter.

"Actually, Alba doesn't have many store-bought toys, she prefers to make her own. We all like to experiment, in fact. Sometimes we find rather strange solutions to our needs. For example, when Alba was just a baby, we didn't have a crib for her, so she slept in a tent. And she loved it! We only changed that when we moved to this house."

Throughout the whole house – in the furniture, objects, materials and colors – a strong duality of influence can be felt. Into the old structure of the house, architectural elements inspired by rationalism have been placed. Alba's bedroom, for instance, has been painted in the colors favored by Le Courbousier, which at the same time evoke nature. Her room is separated from the study area by a unit which on one side acts as her closet, and on the other is a storage space for files. Nearby is a small bathroom with a visible washbasin – "Very practical, I can get water for my paints here!"

The rationalism and abstraction of the architecture contrasts strongly with the omnipresent objects and textures suggesting a much more organic world. Here, a painting with a collection of objects from Chiloé Island, near Patagonia, where legends of the sea abound; there, an untreated wooden bench, Chinese straw sculptures, a cow-hide rug; and the upstairs flooring is of slate.

"We make an effort so that Alba will grow up within both our worlds: the urban, sophisticated world of her mother (from New York) and the rural, wild and earthy culture of her father. The house itself is situated between these extremes. We believe that the child can also be educated by the space around her, by the objects that she sees..."

Hang-it-all. Using the same concept as that which motivates the wire chair, this fixture allows the child to hang any number of things up handily and neatly. With the coloured balls reminding us of jugglers and games, it is a fine example of an object conceived and designed for children that was later adopted by adults.

Designer: Ray and Charles Eames. 1953   Maker: Vitra (Switzerland)   Materials: Metal wire frame with wooden painted balls.   Dimensions: 17 x 50 x 38 cm

Triserre. The Danish designer Nanna Ditzel is of the opinion that a chair for children shouldn't just be a miniature version of an adult chair. We all know that children love to move, fidget and jump up and down; this stool recognises this, and is as much a game as a piece of furniture.

02

Designer: Nanna Ditzel, 1962   Maker: Kvist Mobles (Denmark)   Materials: Solid beechwood   Dimensions: 35 cm in diameter x 28 cm high

Bonito. The traditional gift for the newly born baby in many places is a silver spoon. More than purely symbolic, designed with a use in mind, these pieces of cutlery help the child to learn how to eat. With rounded edges, egonomic handles and a concave fork-spoon to catch falling food. As it is impossible to do a job without the right tools, the knife in this set actually cuts, unlike most 'baby knives'.

03

Designer: Ralph Kramer, 1996   Maker: Pott (Germany)   Materials: Silver or stainless steel.

Tamagó. Meaning 'egg' in Japanese, Tamagó is a symbol of new life and is designed for children from birth to six months. Suggesting at once the shelter of the maternal womb, egg and seed, it is elemental, touching and, in a subtle way, humorous — the sight of baby in this evokes all of these emotions and more.

04

Designer: Lievore Altherr Molina, 1998   Maker: Prenatal (Italy)   Materials: Hardened PVC shell with cotton mattress.   Dimensions: 102 x 85 x 60 cm

16 animales. An open-ended and never-ending incentive to play and learn. Enzo Mari conceived of a game with easily-recognized standing animals at a reasonable price to make and buy. It took him a long time to achieve the effect we have here: that each animal is a version in negative of another. A toy that follows the most venerable of Italian craft traditions, art and cunning design combined.

Designer: Enzo Mari, 1957   Maker: Danese (Italy)   Materials: Resin   Dimensions: 25 x 34.5 cm

Bertoia. A seat designed by the American sculptor Harry Bertoia which evokes the threads of a spiderweb. This design is a reduced-scale version of the original adult type, reflecting the philosophy of the 1950s, which viewed children more as small adults than as developing individuals.

06...

Designer: Harry Bertoia, 1952   Maker: Knoll (USA)   Materials: Frame in polished or matt finish steel. Alternatively, finished in durable nylon coating in black and white.   Dimensions: 40 x 36 x 60 cm (Bertoia Children's Chair #425C) 33 x 31 x 51 cm (Bertoia Baby Chair #426C)

art

expression

Caterina, Domenech. This space is in a rehabilitated medieval building. The house has been reformed and rebuilt many times over the course of the centuries, most recently at the hands of the present owners, both architects. The spaces blend, labyrinth-like, around a patio. Caterina, four, and Domenec, two, share a bedroom, a bathroom, and a games room, an annexe of the living room. Design: Benedetta Tagliabue (Italy) and Enric Miralles (Spain).

The children's bedroom was originally an open space, which was closed off by means of twel[ve] old doors, taken from other parts of the house. The space follows the same stylistic pattern seen in the rest of the house, but includes fascinating details such as the wood and glass do[or] with separable upper and lower sections (for Mom and Dad), and a small window for the ki[ds] to look through.

"We didn't buy much stuff for this room. The huge map of the world was already in the hous[e] and it gave us a kick to hang it up here, where there was a big blank space. The chest of drawers and the table, used as a baby-changing station, was brought in from the study. The on[ly] exception was Caterina's bed, which was one of Enric's special projects. The frame of the b[ed] forms a 'house', and inside the house we installed a toy kitchen for her to play in."

Lelukaappi. The result of the designer's dialogue in miniature with one of Aalvar Aalto's buildings, this model, designed for a civic centre, can be opened and set up as a little theatre. In the words of its designer, the late Enric Miralles, "it is not just a piece of furniture, neither is it merely a building, but as a toy it can be both these things at once, and more."

01

Designer: Enric Miralles & Benedetta Tagliabue Architects, 1996   Materials: Beech plywood   Dimensions: 200 x 30 x 125 cm

"In the beginning, we were planning to paint everything white. But as soon as work began, when we stripped away the wall coverings, the past started to jump out at us from behind them. We found a Gothic archway, an art nouveau room, an eighteenth century fresco –with another, even older, fresco beneath it– and even old brocade wallpaper from the nineteenth century… We came to feel intimately bound up with the past, that all this history around us was ours to claim, and that we were just another link in the chain of time. And so we decided to turn the normal process of historical time on its head. Usually, time is a stratifier, leaving layers of material deposited over the previous strata. We put this into reverse, leaving all the historical layers exposed, so the past could share our living space with us. The compromise we finally reached was to paint everything –walls, windows, doors and furniture, everything– in broad white stripes."

The end result of such a personal interpretation has been to create a densely-layered and highly suggestive ambience, a self-contained world that seems to make no reference to anything outside of itself. The children are of course part of that world, and they leave their own mark on it, but that does not change in the least the individual nature of this home. Rather, the presence of the kids is a logical continuation of that process. For instance, in the short corridor which links the study with the children's bedroom, the worlds of parents and kids meet. Quite spontaneously, this corridor became the 'parking lot' for the toy cars and tractors. And so it happens that in this scene we have, all coexisting in perfect harmony, the eighteenth century fresco, the Eames work seat, and a toy plastic tractor.

"Our thoughts on the house itself have played an important role in our lives and have come to influence our thinking in other projects too. We began to think of it somewhat as you would think of a set of silver cutlery given to you as a wedding gift. Kept in a drawer, these things are completely useless; to be of value to you, you really have to use them every day. Our home is very far from being an abstract concept for us; on the contrary, it's a place where we feel we can truly live."

Baby Crosby Chair. Gaetano Pesce came to fame in the 1970s for his deconstructivist and experimental use of plastic. In this chair, as with most of his objects, we have the spontaneity of a child's imagination, with no thought for commercial effect. Childish and childlike, it is perforated and coloured with apparent randomness.

02

Designer: Gaetano Pesce, 1999   Maker: De Padova (Italy)   Materials: Colored translucent resin   Dimensions: 41 x 30 x 53 cm

Eternal Circle. To make this baby's rattle toy, the jewelry designer Elsa Peretti chose a symbol from her personal universe, especially fitting for a new-born baby: the eternal circle. Neither too heavy for little hands, nor so small that it could be swallowed, this object was produced at the request of the designer's friends. The whole is made in a special non-toxic silver. Both plaything and art object.

03

Designer: Elsa Perreti, 1988-1990   Maker: Tiffany's (USA)   Material: Silver   Dimensions: 6cm in diameter

Walnut Stools. A museum curator ordered two of these fine pieces of furniture for his children. "Graduation present, I suppose?" said the salesman. "No," said the client, "They are just three and five years old right now. It's just that I want them to grow up with a piece of true quality that will last them all their lives." This object, a personal favourite of the designers, can also form a bedside table.

04

Designer: Ray and Charles Eames, 1960   Maker: Vitra (Switzerland)   Materials: Solid walnut wood   Dimensions: 33 cm in diameter x 38 cm high

Je préfère ma maman. A baby's feeding bottle with a sly, ironic message from the French artist Ben, working as always in stark black and white. With witty phrases in chalkboard style scrawled all over the bottle, the artist comments, with a knowing wink to contemporary parents, on the ambiguities and guilt pangs of being an independent working mother.

05...

Designer: Ben, 1998   Maker: Blayo (France)   Materials: Unbreakable plastic suitable for sterilizer, color coating. Silicon teat.   Dimensions: 4.5 cm in diameter x 20 cm high

function

nature

Bernat, Pau. Bernat, Pau. The present family of owners - the mother an interior designer and the father a communications consultant - have entirely reformed this rural house, starting from a disused stable of which only the outer walls and the roof survived. Bernat, eight, and his brother Pau, five, share a tiny room where there is only just enough space for a bunk bed, a closet and a small attic space with a mattress for a friend to sleep over. Design: Carlos Pibernat, Mariona Soler, Jordi Parcerisas (Spain)

"We live in the city, but we have a strong urge to get out of there and experience life in the country. What's more, we have a lot of friends and relatives in this area, so we come out here practically every weekend. This is where we live a simpler, more relaxed life. People drop by, we improvise a big meal together, we head off to the beach... It's also a great thing for the kids, they get to ride their bikes, go picking firewood in the forest, and they can drop in on our neighbours - a family of farmers, where the kids can do such fascinating stuff as pet cows, ride tractors, feed the lambs and chickens, and so on."

The boys spend all day playing either outside or in the ground floor space, largely open, with the kitchen on one side and the living area on the other. Upstairs are the bedrooms and bathrooms. Since the ground floor is one continuous space, the flooring is especially tough hardened concrete which can withstand the worst from bicycles, tricycles and even the old toy car, purchased in Holland. The closet space here is shared: above, plates and saucers; below, toys, paper and paints. In the summer this is an exterior space, so the materials here are robust, resistant and natural.

Whenever weather permits, the family's life takes place outdoors. Out on the terrace, beneath a bower of wisteria, barbecues are held on folding chairs and tables and people sleep off their lunch by napping on hammocks strung between the trees. The garden forms a great rectangle, contained between the facade, the lateral garden walls, and the field at the bottom, facing the house.

Paysage inondable. A dish which is a 'mini-landscape'. It holds a country cottage, able to withstand storms of spaghetti or blizzards of yogurt. Ideal for stimulating the child's appetite with dinnertime stories.

01

Designer: Patrick Martinez, 1997   Maker: Axis (France)   Materials: Ceramic, various colors available   Dimensions: 22 cm diameter x 4 cm high

The mantle at the rear of the ground floor area is placed at such a height that it can serve simultaneously as a low surface, a prolongation of the fireplace, or as a drawing desk for the boys

The children's room is quite simple by necessity: only the bunk bed and a recessed closet will fit in this space. On the other side of the window is a narrow wooden ladder which leads up to a small attic space, containing a mattress for small guests and a chest for toys and books. As the boys use the room only to sleep, no more space or features are needed here. The space thus saved on their room is employed for a spare room, which serves both as a guest room and to insulate the parents' and children's rooms acoustically.

Stockwekbett. Manufactured in the same formally timeless and tender design since 1965, this bunk bed offers a wealth of possibilities for the imagination, be it shop, castle or pirate ship. Simply by removing the posts connecting the bunks, the beds become two singles.

Designer: Elis Borg, 1965   Maker: Steybe (Germany)   Materials: Solid birchwood frame, treated with non-toxic preparations
Dimensions: 219 x 103 x 170 cm

And it is here, at the entrance to the property, that we find the feature which is every child's dream (and every adult's too): a treehouse, high up in the branches, at a 'safe distance' from the house and with a splendid view of the country and the roads around.

"We made it with some friends, making use of timber left over from the work on the house. We refused to buy anything else for it. It's an old dream of ours come true for the children – though we adults must own up to using it too. In fact, sometimes the grown-ups go up to the treehouse to get away from the noisy kids! It's a great spot for a view of the house, above all at night. I sit there in the darkness, smoke a cigarette, and I watch the house as if it were a big cinema screen, with a story appearing in every window."

Tweeler y Twinstar. This toy, a bicycle in structure but with the pedaling action of a tricycle, makes it easy for kids to learn to ride a bike. The true three-wheel version has the added advantage of allowing its owner to attach a trailer, becoming the ideal vehicle for transporting friends or toys from one place to another. Since they are built robust enough for the demands of kindergartens and playgroups, they are perfect for home use too.

Designer: Community Playthings   Maker: Community Playthings (UK)   Materials: Lightweight frame of solid steel, painted. Plastic seat and pedals. Protected wheels.   Dimensions: 88 cm length, 38 cm seat height (Tweeler)

Sleepi. A moses-basket for new-born babies which can be converted into a cradle with bars. Later on, opening up the bed and lowering the mattress, the bed can be used up to three or four years of age. Truly versatile, it can also be transformed into a two-level house, two separate chairs, a sofa, or a chair-table combination.

04

Designer: Susanne Gronlund, Klaus Hviid Knudsen .1998   Maker: Stokke (Norway)   Materials: Solid and laminated beechwood frame, with optional varnish or wax-effect finish. Cotton coverings and side protector band.   Dimensions: 126 x 73 x 94 cm

Sand and Water Table. Based around a mobile table - when the cover is taken off, we reveal a water container and sand table. Several children can play at once around this table, just the thing for a rainy day when playing outdoors is impossible.

05

Designer: Community Playthings   Maker: Community Playthings (UK)   Materials: Frame and cover in wood with resistant transparent polyurethane coating. Water container in red and white PVC, equipped with hose outlet for draining into sink.   Dimensions: 120 x 60 x 60 cm (also available with height 45 cm)

Vaca y Vaquita. Originally it was conceived as an ergonomic work-chair which obliged the user to change posture every so often, becoming the focus for an interesting game. Equipped with horns and wheels, and covered in genuine cowhide, it's all you need to set up a mini-rodeo at home.

Designer: Michael Lehner, 1995   **Maker:** Freiraum (Germany)   **Materials:** Foam rubber with cowhide cover, fur horns, industrial rollers
Dimensions: 47 x 74 x 52 cm (Vaca) and 29 x 44 x 37 cm (Vaquita)

experiment

perspective

Álvaro, Juanito. This is a five-storey house located in a town close to the city and designed entirely by the owners, both architects. Their two children, Álvaro aged eight and Juanito aged nine, share a bedroom and a bathroom. Designers: Teresa Rumeu and Íñigo Gurrea (Spain)

Juanito drew this picture just after his father died. He called it "A Man's Life", and it shows a baby being born in hospital, then childhood – a baby carriage, a visit to an exhibition, a school, a fight – then how the child becomes a big, strong man, and how the man becomes small and weak again. Finally we see his grave, with the inscription "To my loved ones". When he drew this he was six years old.

May Day. The name of this product is an allusion to the emergency lamps on board ships. This item was not designed for children, though it easily could have been, as it is practically unbreakable and is very versatile in use. You can hang it up, lay it down, stand it on the floor or carry it with you wherever you need it. An object that yearns to give you a helping hand.

01

Designer: Constanin Grcic, 1998   Maker: Flos (Italy)   Materials: Polypropylene   Dimensions: 22 cm in diameter, 53 cm in height

TorreDin. Initially developed for an artist's studio, these wooden containers are useful for storing all kinds of things, offering order and an aesthetic pleasure in the dialogue between the different sizes . A simple solution for storage needs, transformed at the same time into something almost sculptural in value.

02

Designer: Martin Azúa, Ronan Boroullec, Jean François Dingjan, 1998   Maker: Martin Azúa   Materials: Birch ply   Dimensions: Five sizes, based on paper sizes A1 to A4. When stacked, they measure 90 x 60 x 120 cm

However, most of the time the boys do their homework in the kitchen-dining area, which includes a sofa and behind it photos and the children's artwork hung on the wall. In summer, this space extends into the patio, where there is a swimming pool with more than a passing resemblance to a great bathtub. "Right now, this is the boys' space, not mine. They play basketball and handball here, so it would be impossible for me to plant a garden - in the future, perhaps, I'll have plants here, but this is their time."

The children and their dog run noisily upstairs and downstairs, there is the clatter of skateboards and bikes, and everywhere you go there seems to be a PC in a corner - either for games, or work or for study. It is a lively, glowing and functioning place, where the environment if full of energy, curiosity and hope for the future.

Pisoló. A 'surprise bed' for friends or babysitters to stay in overnight. In the container is a complete inflatable bed, equipped with a powerful mini-air pump which inflates it for you in a few seconds. It takes up hardly any space, and can function as a bedside table. As children are always enchanted by the "jack-in-the-box" effect, they may well end up wanting to sleep in this bed instead of the guest, as intended.

03

Designer: Denis Santachiara, 1997 Maker: Campeggi (Italy) Materials: PVC and polyeurathane with reversible lycra cover Dimensions: 83 x 190 cm (inflated)

Mr. Pook. An electric toothbrush designed to encourage children to build the teeth-cleaning habit. A Tamagotchi-sized electronic screen displays a happy white tooth, which becomes blackened and miserable after going for 12 hours without use. When the brush is in use, the tooth dances and sings with joy. An attractive and charming way to learn a healthy habit.

04

Designer: Emma Lipschutz, Margarita Navarro, Einav Sadan, 2000   Materials: ABS plastic and injected foam rubber   Dimensions: Brush 3 cm in diameter, 18 cm high; support/recharger 5.5 x 6 x 7.5 cm

Floppy. Sofabed for guests, bench or play area? All three and more. A conceptual piece, in contemporary form, and so simple to set up that children can do it unaided by adults.

Designer: Tim Power, 1989   Maker: BRF (Italy)   Materials: Foam rubber, with cover.   Dimensions: 200 x 100 cm

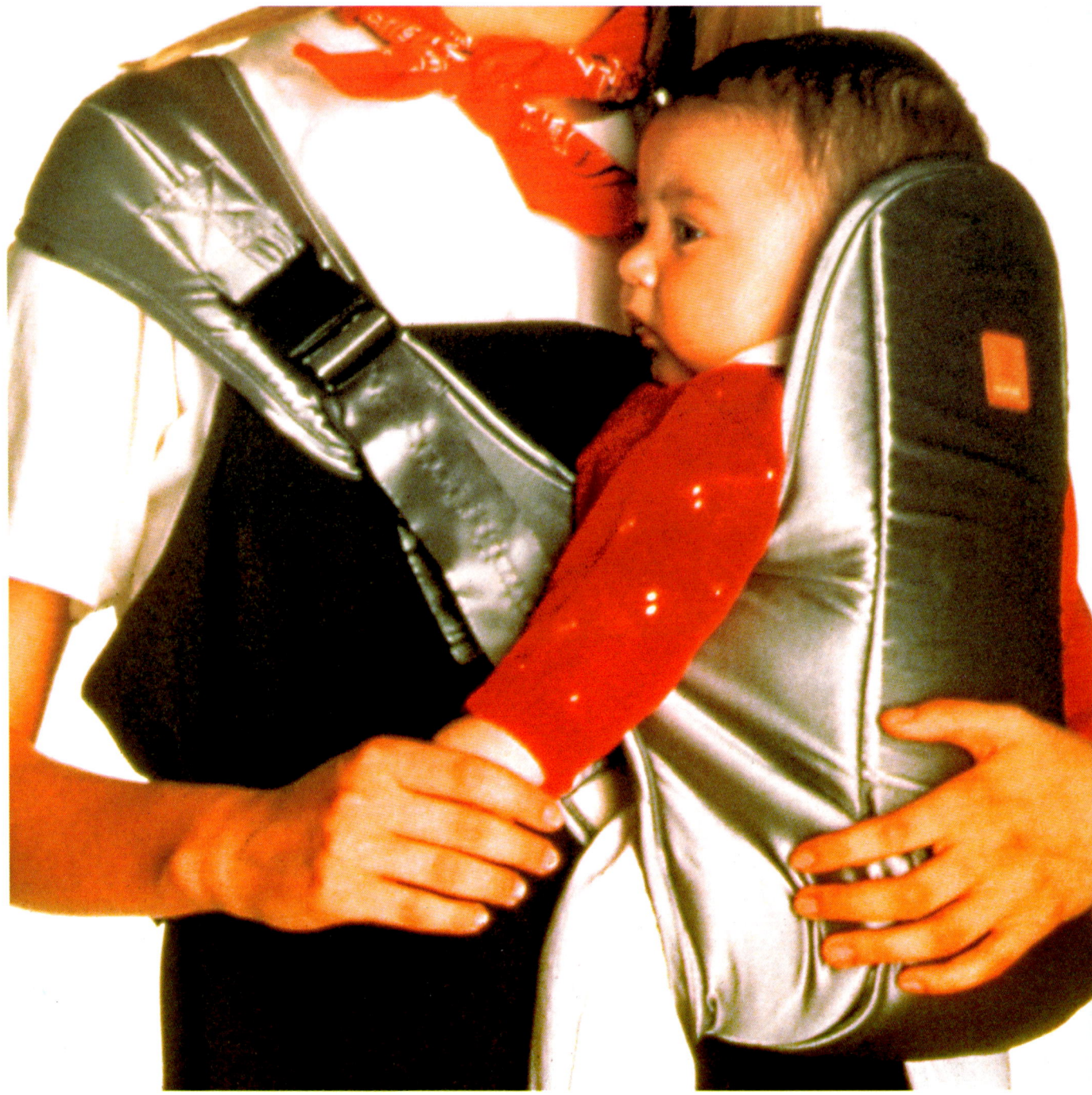

Baby Carrier. Allowing the parent to hold the child close while keeping hands free, this sling preserves that crucial physical contact at all times. The baby can be carried on the chest up to about three or four months, then is carried supported on the hips up to 18 months. The result of rigorous testing, a superb contemporary adaptation of a traditional way of carrying young children.

Designer: Terry Decora and Marian de Rond, 1996   Maker Prenatal (Italy)   Material: Light washable 100% cotton, available in blue and silver
Dimensions: 91 x 52 x 55 cm

AGUADÉ   Passatge de l'Ensenyança 17   08013 Barcelona / Spain   tel.+fax 93 427 54 69

AMAT 3   Cami Can Blos, 5-7   08760 Martorell / Spain   tel.34 93 775 56 51   fax 34 93 775 34 54   amat@amat-3.com   amat-3.com

Katrin Arens   Via per i Molini di sotto   24030 Pontida   tel.+fax. 035783336   katrin.arens @uninetcom.it

ARTEK   Eteläesplanadi 18   00130 Helsinki / Finland   Södra esplanaden18   00130 Helsingfors   tel. 358 9 613 250   fax 358 9 61 32 52 60

ART & FORM snc   Corso Sicilia 17   10133 Torino   tel. 01 16 61 46 44   fax 01 16 61 47 87

AXIS   tel. 01 46 77 63 60   fax 01 46 78 54 19   axis_fr@compuserve.com

BLAYO   7, Ter rue du Dr. Arnaudet   92190 Meudon / France   tel. 0033 1 45 34 07 00   fax 00 33 1 45 34 75 00   yblayo@aol.com

BRF snc/ Italia   Loc. S Narziale 21   53034 Colle val d1Elsa   tel. 0577 92 94 18   fax 0577929648   www.brfcolors.com   biancucci@brfcolors.com

B & T   Calle Saclosa 4   08240 Manresa / Spain   tel. 93872 50 28   fax 93872 19 53

Marta Rodriguez Boix   Barcelona/ Spain   tel+fax 93 268 30 52

CAMPEGGI srl   Via del Cavolto 8   33044 Anzano del Parco (CO) / Italy   tel. 03 163 04 95   fax 03 163 22 05   www.campeggi.it

COMMUNITY PLAYTHINGS   Darvell Robertsbridge   East Sussex / UK TN 32 5 DR   tel. 0800 387 457   fax 0800387 531

DANESE srl   Via Canova 34   20 145 Milano / Italia   tel. 02 349 39 534   fax 02 345 38 211   www.danesemilano.com   info@danesemilano.com

DE PADOVA srl   Corso Venezia 14   20121 Milano / Italy   tel. 02 77 72 01   fax 02 77 72 02 80   www.depadova.it   clienti@depadova.it

DROOG DESIGN LIMITED   Parkweg 14   2271 Aj Voorburg / The Netherlands   tel. 70 386 40 38   fax 70 387 30 75

DOMODINAMICA MODULAR srl   Via Molise, 23   40060 Osteria Grande (Bologna) / Italy   tel. 0519 45 896   fax. 050 94 58 53   www.domodinamica.com   modular@domodinamica.com

DOMOVITAL   Kolpingweg 4   48720 Rosendahl / Dahrenfeld / Germany   tel. 02545 / 91960   fax 02545 / 919610   e-mail: info@domovital.com   www.domovital.com

FREIRAUM   Bahnhofsplatz 1   82319 Starnberg / Alemania

FLOS spa   Via Angelo Faini 2   25073 Bovezzo BS   tel.03 02 43 81   fax. 03 02 43 82 50   www.flos.it

FLOU spa   via Cadorna, 12   20036 Meda (MI) / Italy   tel. 0362 37 31   fax 036 27 48 01   www.flou.it

FORNASETTI IMMAGINAZIONE srl   Via Bazzini 14   20 131Milano / Italy   tel. 02 2666341 - 70601734   fax 02 270601130

GUNTHER LAMBERT GmbH   Konstantinstr. 303   41238 Mönchengladbach / Germany   t 021 66 86 83 0   f 021 66 86 83 39   office@gunther-lambert.com   www.gunther-lambert.com

HUGO POTT GmbH   Ritterstr. 28   42659 Solingen / Germany   t 0212 43056   f 0212 42425   www.pott-bestecke.de   pott@pott-bestecke.de

ITALTRIKE   Via dell1Artigianato 30   San Zenone degli Ezzelini (TV) / Italy   tel. 0423 56 79 55   fax 0423 56 79 07   italtrike@prometeo.com

KINNASAND   Danzigerstr. 6   26655 Westerstede / Germany   tel. 044 88 / 516 24   fax 044 88 / 516 16   design@kinnasand.de

KNOLL INTERNATIONAL   www.knoll.com

KVIST MOBLER A/S   Siggardsvej 2   6818 Arre / Denmark

MALOFANCON   Via Cardinale de Lai, 10   36034 Maio (Vicenza) / Italy   tel. 0445 60 246   fax 0445 58 00 32

NANI MARQUINA   Distribuidor: Mobles 114   Enric Granados 114   08008 Barcelona / Spain   tel. 93 260 01 14   fax 93 237 13 65

ORIZZONTI   Gruppo I.C.A.   Via Birago. 10   20020 Misinto / Italy   tel. 02 967 20 763   fax 02 967 20 444

RÉNATAL / Italy   magaboa@tin.it

SELLEX   Donosti Ibilbidea, 84   Polígono 26   20115 Astigarraga (Guipuzkoa) / Spain   tel. 943 55 70 11   fax 943 55 70 50   www.sellex.es   sellex@adegi.es

TEYBE   Fellbacherstrass. 54   73 630 Remshalden-Grunbach / Germany   tel. 00 49 7151.731.73   fax 00 49 7151. 731.33

STOKKE DENMARK A/S   6260 Skodje / Noruega   tel. 47 70 24 00   fax 47 70 24 49 90   www.stokke.com   info@stokke.com

TIFFANY & CO   5th Avenue and 57th Street   NY 10022 NY / USA   tel. 800 526 06 49   www.tiffany.com

Gebrüder THONET GmbH   Postfach 1520   Michael Thonet Strasse 1   35066 Frankemberg / Germany   tel. 06451/ 508 0   fax 06451/ 508 108   info@ thonet.de   www.thonet.de

VITRA / Suissa   info@vitra.com   www.vitra.com

My deepest thanks go to: Julia Schulz-Dornberg, for her invaluable help and support; Olga Carretero for her sensitive gaze; Laura Amet for her fine graphic work, superb cooking and calming presence; Teresa Ricart for her verbal ingenuity and untiring good humor; and Bernardo Quirogo for his rigour and the patience of a saint. Thanks also to all the children we've visited and photographed, to their parents, and to all who have helped in the completion of this task.